By the Editors of Best Recipes

Best Recipes

DESSERTS

COOKBOOK

SMITHMARK

This edition published in 1991 by SMITHMARK Publishers Inc., 112 Madison Avenue, New York, NY 10016.

SMITHMARK books are available for bulk purchase for sales promotion and premium use. For details write or telephone the Manager of Special Sales, SMITHMARK Publishers Inc., 112 Madison Avenue, New York, NY 10016. (212) 532-6600.

Photography on pages 29, 79 and 89 by Vuksanovich/Chicago.

Photography on page 59 by Burke/Triolo Studio/Los Angeles.

Remaining photography by Sacco Productions Limited/Chicago.
Photographers: Ray Cheydler
　　　　　　　Warren Hansen
　　　　　　　Laurie Proffitt
Photo Stylists/Production: Betty Karslake
　　　　　　　　　　　　　Paula Walters
Food Stylists: Lois Hlavac
　　　　　　　Carol Parik

ISBN: 0-8317-0599-X

Library of Congress Catalog Card Number: 90-6443

Pictured on the front cover: The Golden Strawberry (*page 64*).

Pictured on the back cover (*clockwise from top left*): Pineapple Macadamia Cheesepie (*page 68*), Grand Marnier Brownies (*page 42*), Mixed Berry Pie (*page 14*) and Angel Cream Dessert (*page 80*).

First published in the United States.

Manufactured in Yugoslavia.

8　7　6　5　4　3　2　1

By the Editors of Best Recipes

Best Recipes

DESSERTS

COOKBOOK

DESSERT BASICS

A fabulous dessert adds a special touch to any meal and this collection is sure to please. You'll marvel at the variety of desserts—cakes, pies, souffle's, mousses, even a cookie or two—and the multitude of flavors like vanilla, caramel, cherry, peanut butter, apple, strawberry, maple and of course chocolate!

This unique collection of award-winning desserts will provide you with wonderful treats to top off a delicious dinner or for anytime you want to serve something special. Gathered from cooking contests across America, it represents some of the very best offerings in delightful desserts—original recipes created by home cooks like you. The names of these champion cooks as well as the contests they entered are included for each and every delectable creation.

Success in the kitchen is often a matter of careful organization and preparation. Before you begin a recipe, read through the instructions carefully and gather all the ingredients and equipment. Do not make substitutions for ingredients unless specifically called for in the recipe. Substitutions can alter the delicate balance of ingredients and the result may be less than perfect. Mastering the following dessert-making skills will help ensure success every time.

Baking Tips
—Measure all ingredients carefully and accurately. To measure flour, spoon lightly into a dry measuring cup and level off with the flat edge of a knife (do not shake it down or tap it on the counter).
—Use the pan size specified in each recipe and prepare it as stated. The wrong size pan may cause a burned bottom and edges or a sunken middle.
—Oven temperatures can vary significantly depending on the oven model and manufacturer, so watch your dessert carefully and check for doneness using the test given in the recipe.

Pastry Making Tips
—Cut the shortening, margarine or butter into the flour and salt using a pastry blender or two knives until the crumbs resemble small peas. Add the liquid, 1 tablespoon at a time, tossing lightly with a fork, until the dough is just moist enough to hold together when pressed.
—If the dough is sticky and difficult to handle, refrigerate it until firm. Flour the rolling pin and surface just enough to prevent sticking. Handle the dough quickly and lightly. A tough pie crust is often the result of too much flour worked into the dough and overhandling it.

—Roll the dough out to a circle 1 inch larger than an inverted pie plate. Carefully fold the dough into quarters and place it in the pie plate. Unfold it and gently press into place. Be careful not to pull or stretch the dough, as this will cause it to shrink during baking.

—Often a pie shell will be "baked blind" or baked before the filling is added. In order to keep the pastry from puffing up during baking, line the shell with foil and weigh it down with dried beans, uncooked rice or ceramic or metal pie weights. Bake the shell until set; remove the foil and weights and cool completely before adding filling.

Beating Egg Whites

—Be sure to refrigerate all egg-based desserts as soon as possible and keep them chilled.

—Eggs will separate more easily when cold, but egg whites will reach their fullest volume if allowed to stand at room temperature for 30 minutes before beating.

—When beating egg whites, always check that your bowl and beaters are completely clean and dry. The smallest trace of yolk, water or fat can interfere with obtaining maximum volume. For best results, use a copper, stainless steel or glass bowl (plastic bowls may have an oily film, even after repeated washings).

—Beat the whites slowly until they are foamy, then increase the speed. Add a pinch of salt and cream of tartar at this point to help stabilize them. Do not overbeat or they will become dry and clump together.

—Immediately fold beaten egg whites gently into another mixture so volume is not lost; never beat or stir.

Dissolving Gelatin

—To dissolve gelatin successfully, sprinkle one package of gelatin over ¼ cup of cold liquid in a small saucepan. Let it stand for 1 minute to soften. Stir over low heat until the gelatin is completely dissolved, about 5 minutes.

—Run a finger over the spoon to test for undissolved granules. If it is smooth, the gelatin is completely dissolved; if it feels granular, continue heating until it feels smooth.

—Fresh, uncooked pineapple, papaya and kiwifruit contain enzymes that prevent gelatin from becoming firm. Boil these fruits for 2 minutes before adding to a gelatin mixture.

Whipping Cream

—For best results when beating heavy or whipping cream, chill the cream, bowl and beaters first—the cold keeps the fat in the cream solid, thus increasing the volume.

—For optimum volume, beat the cream in a deep, narrow bowl. Generally 1 cup of cream will yield 2 cups of whipped cream so be sure to choose a bowl that will accommodate the increased volume. Do not overbeat or the cream will clump together and form butter.

Melting Chocolate

—To melt chocolate, place chips or chopped chocolate pieces in a clean, dry, heavy saucepan. Heat over low heat until melted and smooth, stirring constantly. Or, place the chocolate in the top of a double boiler over hot (not boiling) water, stirring until smooth.

—To melt chocolate in the microwave, place 8 to 12 ounces of chopped chocolate in a dry microwaveable container. Microwave at HIGH 1 minute; stir well. Microwave at HIGH for an additional 30 to 60 seconds until smooth, stirring twice.

PERFECT PIES

Making Chocolate Curls

Melt chocolate in the top of a double boiler over hot water, stirring frequently. Pour the melted chocolate onto a cold baking sheet and spread thinly into a rectangle. Refrigerate just until set, about 15 minutes. Pull the long edge of a long metal spatula across the surface of the soft chocolate, letting it curl up in front of the spatula. Place the curls on waxed paper.

White Russian Pie

♦ Virgel Kelly Jr. won first prize in the Knox® Unflavored Gelatine "Just Desserts" Recipe Contest sponsored by Thomas J. Lipton, Inc.

Makes 6 to 8 servings

  2 cups chocolate wafer crumbs
  5 tablespoons butter or margarine, melted
  7 tablespoons coffee liqueur, divided
  1 envelope Knox® Unflavored Gelatine
  6 tablespoons sugar, divided
  3 eggs,* separated
  ½ cup water
  ¼ cup vodka
  1 cup whipping cream, whipped
    Chocolate curls, for garnish

Preheat oven to 350°F. Combine crumbs, butter and 4 tablespoons of the coffee liqueur in small bowl. Press firmly on bottom and up side of 9-inch pie plate. Bake 3 minutes; cool completely on wire rack.

Combine gelatine and 4 tablespoons of the sugar in medium saucepan. Stir in egg yolks and water; let stand 1 minute. Stir over low heat until gelatine is completely dissolved, about 5 minutes. Stir in vodka and remaining 3 tablespoons coffee liqueur. Turn into large bowl and refrigerate, stirring occasionally, until mixture mounds slightly when dropped from spoon.

Beat egg whites in medium bowl until soft peaks form; gradually add remaining 2 tablespoons sugar and beat until stiff and glossy. Fold into gelatine mixture. Fold in whipped cream. Turn into prepared crust; refrigerate until firm. Garnish with chocolate curls.

*Use clean, uncracked eggs.

Crisp, tart, juicy Granny Smith apples are not only delicious eaten raw, but are also excellent for baking because they keep their texture. And unlike other apples, you can enjoy these green-skinned beauties year-round. After the fall American-grown crop is consumed, the harvest from New Zealand and Australia arrives in spring.

My Golden Harvest Apple Pie

♦ Charlotte Granville from Manchester, Connecticut was the Connecticut representative at the Crisco® American Pie Celebration National Bake-Off, Los Angeles, California.

Makes 6 to 8 servings

Classic Crisco® Double Crust (see page 14)
2 tablespoons all-purpose flour
½ cup sugar
1 teaspoon ground cinnamon
1 teaspoon ground nutmeg
5 to 6 cups peeled and thinly sliced apples*
**   (about 2 pounds)**
3 tablespoons low-sugar orange marmalade
2 tablespoons butter or margarine
Milk

Prepare pie crust. Sprinkle with flour; set aside. Preheat oven to 450°F. Combine sugar, cinnamon and nutmeg in small bowl. Layer apple slices alternately with sugar mixture in pie crust. Press down gently to eliminate air pockets. Dot with marmalade and butter.

Roll out remaining half of dough to circle 1 inch larger than pie plate. Place over apples. Fold edge under; flute. Cut slits or design for steam to escape. Brush top crust with milk. If desired, reroll dough scraps and cut into decorative shapes. Bake 15 minutes. *Reduce oven temperature to 375°F.* Continue baking 30 to 35 minutes or until golden brown. Cool completely on wire rack.

*For spectacular results use half Golden Delicious apples and half tart, firm apples such as Stayman, Northern Spy, Granny Smith or Winesap.

Lemons are rarely eaten on their own, but they are probably used more than any other fruit, in everything from flavoring beverages and pies to adding zest to vegetables, fish and poultry. They can even prevent some fruits (such as apples and bananas) from turning brown when sliced. Fresh lemons are found in supermarkets year-round and bottled lemon juice is also widely available. To get the most juice from your lemons, warm to room temperature and press down as you roll them on the countertop with the palm of your hand before squeezing. To remove peel in strips, use a very sharp knife or vegetable peeler (or a special gadget called a lemon zester). Remove only the colored part of the peel. If necessary, scrape any white left on peels before adding to recipe.

Heavenly Sinful Lemon Chiffon Pie

♦ Toni Canfill was the second place winner in the Junior division of the Citrus Pie Contest at the National Orange Show, San Bernardino, California.

Makes one 9-inch pie

CRUST
 1 cup all-purpose flour
 ¼ cup sugar
 1 tablespoon grated lemon peel
 ½ cup butter
 1 egg yolk, slightly beaten
 ½ teaspoon vanilla
 1 teaspoon lemon juice

FILLING
 4 eggs,* separated
 1 cup sugar, divided
 ⅓ cup lemon juice
 2 tablespoons grated lemon peel
 ½ teaspoon unflavored gelatin
 ¼ teaspoon salt
 Whipped cream and lemon peel, for garnish

Preheat oven to 400°F. To make crust, combine flour, ¼ cup sugar and 1 tablespoon lemon peel in medium bowl. Cut in butter until mixture resembles coarse crumbs. Stir in egg yolk, vanilla and 1 teaspoon lemon juice. Press evenly in 9-inch pie plate; trim and flute edge. Prick dough and line with foil. Fill with dried beans, uncooked rice or pie weights and bake 10 minutes. Remove foil lining and beans; cool completely on wire rack.

To make filling, beat 4 egg yolks in small bowl. Combine with ½ cup of the sugar, ⅓ cup lemon juice, 2 tablespoons lemon peel and the gelatin in top of double boiler. Cook over boiling water 5 minutes or until thickened, stirring constantly. Remove from heat. Beat egg whites and salt in large bowl until soft peaks form. Gradually add remaining ½ cup sugar, beating until stiff and glossy. Fold egg white mixture into lemon mixture; pour into cooled crust. Refrigerate until set. Garnish with whipped cream and lemon peel.

Use clean, uncracked eggs.

Golden Ambrosia Pecan Pie

♦ Mary Louise Lever from Rome, Georgia was the Georgia representative at the Crisco® American Pie Celebration National Bake-Off, Atlanta, Georgia.

Makes 6 to 8 servings

1 Classic Crisco® Single Crust
  (recipe follows)
3 eggs, beaten
¾ cup light corn syrup
½ cup granulated sugar
3 tablespoons packed brown sugar
2 tablespoons butter or margarine, melted
3 tablespoons thawed orange juice concentrate
2 tablespoons cornstarch
1 teaspoon grated orange peel
1 teaspoon vanilla
½ teaspoon coconut flavoring or extract
1½ cups chopped pecans
⅔ cup flaked coconut

Prepare pie crust; set aside. Preheat oven to 350°F. Combine eggs, corn syrup, granulated sugar, brown sugar and butter in large bowl; mix well. Combine orange juice concentrate, cornstarch, orange peel, vanilla and coconut flavor; add to egg mixture, stirring until well blended. Stir in pecans and flaked coconut. Pour into prepared pie crust. Cover edge with foil to prevent overbrowning.

Bake 35 minutes; remove foil. Return to oven for 15 to 20 minutes or until set. Cool completely on wire rack.

Classic Crisco® Single Crust
1⅓ cups all-purpose flour
  ½ teaspoon salt
  ½ cup Butter Flavor Crisco®
  5 tablespoons cold water

Combine flour and salt in medium bowl. Cut in shortening until mixture resembles coarse crumbs. Sprinkle water, 1 tablespoon at a time, over flour mixture and toss with fork until mixture holds together. Press together to form ball. Roll out dough on lightly floured surface to circle 1 inch larger than inverted 9-inch pie plate. Press into pie plate; trim and flute edge or reroll dough scraps and form decorative border.

Pecans are native to America and grown in the South and Southwest. Next to the peanut, it is the most popular nut in the United States. Although pecans are often baked into cookies and cakes and eaten as a snack, they are at their most sublime when baked into a pie. Pecan pie is made with a corn syrup custard to which the nuts are added. When the pie has cooled, serve it wreathed in a cloud of whipped cream. Or, serve it warm with vanilla ice cream on the side.

The food processor can make a delightful pastry dough in a very short time. Be sure the shortening is fully chilled (put in the freezer for 15 to 20 minutes if desired). Combine the flour and salt and add half of the shortening. Process with quick pulses until the mixture resembles coarse crumbs. Add the remaining shortening and repeat the process. Quickly add the ice water through the feed tube while pulsing; stop as soon as the dough looks like it will gather into a ball. Gather it into a ball and refrigerate before rolling out.

Mixed Berry Pie

♦ Sue Rice from Schell City, Missouri was the Missouri representative at the Crisco® American Pie Celebration National Finals, Los Angeles, California.

Makes 6 to 8 servings

Classic Crisco® Double Crust (recipe follows)
2 cups canned or frozen blackberries, thawed and well drained
1½ cups canned or frozen blueberries, thawed and well drained
½ cup canned or frozen gooseberries, thawed and well drained
¼ cup sugar
3 tablespoons cornstarch
⅛ teaspoon almond extract

Prepare pie crust; set aside. Preheat oven to 425°F. Combine blackberries, blueberries and gooseberries in large bowl. Add sugar, cornstarch and almond extract; stir well. Spoon into prepared pie crust. Roll out remaining half of dough to circle 1 inch larger than pie plate. Place over filling. Fold edge under; flute. Cut slits or design for steam to escape. Bake 40 minutes or until crust is golden brown. Cool completely on wire rack.

Classic Crisco® Double Crust
2 cups all-purpose flour
1 teaspoon salt
¾ cup Crisco® Shortening
5 tablespoons cold water

Combine flour and salt in large bowl. Cut in shortening until mixture resembles coarse crumbs. Gradually add water, 1 tablespoon at a time; toss with fork until mixture holds together. Press together to form ball. Divide dough in half. Roll out half of dough on lightly floured surface to circle 1 inch larger than inverted 9-inch pie plate. Press in pie plate. Wrap remaining dough in plastic wrap; set aside.

Norma Gene's Peanut Butter Creme Pie

♦ Norma Gene Anderson from Crete, Nebraska was a finalist in the Miscellaneous Cream Pie category at the Nebraska State Fair, Lincoln, Nebraska.

Makes 6 to 8 servings

1 9-inch unbaked single pie crust*
¾ cup granulated sugar, divided
3 tablespoons cornstarch
1 tablespoon all-purpose flour
⅛ teaspoon salt
3 eggs, separated
3 cups milk
2 teaspoons butter or margarine
1 teaspoon vanilla
½ cup crunchy peanut butter
¾ cup powdered sugar
¼ teaspoon cream of tartar

Preheat oven to 425°F. Prick dough and line with foil. Fill with dried beans, uncooked rice or pie weights; bake 10 to 15 minutes or until lightly brown. Remove foil and beans. Cool completely on wire rack. In 2-quart saucepan, stir together ½ cup of the granulated sugar, the cornstarch, flour and salt. Add egg yolks and milk; stir with wire whisk until well blended. Bring to a boil over medium heat, stirring constantly. Continue cooking and stirring 2 minutes or until thick. Remove from heat. Stir in butter and vanilla.

Reduce oven temperature to 375°F. Cut peanut butter into powdered sugar until mixture resembles coarse crumbs. Sprinkle ⅓ of the peanut butter crumbs over bottom of pie crust. Spoon ½ of the milk mixture over crumbs. Sprinkle with another ⅓ of the crumbs, top with remaining pudding. Combine cream of tartar and egg whites in medium bowl. Beat egg whites at high speed until soft peaks form. Gradually add remaining ¼ cup granulated sugar, beating until stiff and glossy. Spread over pudding and seal to edge of crust. Sprinkle remaining peanut butter crumbs around edge. Bake 8 to 10 minutes or until meringue is golden. Cool completely on wire rack.

*Use your favorite pie crust recipe or see page 12.

Brown sugar is a mixture of granulated sugar and molasses that adds a rich flavor to baked goods. Dark brown sugar has more molasses added and will actually give foods a darker color. Light brown sugar has a milder flavor and lighter color than the dark variety. Whatever the type, brown sugar is moist and clingy when fresh but can easily dry out. Adding a slice of apple or bread to the box or bag will restore moisture.

Topsy Turvy Apple Pie

♦ Beverly McDevitt from Livonia, Michigan was a finalist in the General Public category of the Apple-Cooking Cooking Contest, sponsored by the Michigan Apple Committee, DeWitt, Michigan.

Makes 6 to 8 servings

1 unbaked 9-inch double pie crust*
¼ cup butter or margarine, softened
½ cup pecan halves
½ cup packed brown sugar
4 large Granny Smith apples, peeled, cored and sliced
1 tablespoon lemon juice
1 tablespoon all-purpose flour
½ cup granulated sugar
1 teaspoon ground cinnamon
1 teaspoon ground nutmeg
Dash of salt

Preheat oven to 400°F. Roll out half of pie crust dough on lightly floured surface to circle 1 inch larger than inverted pie plate. Set aside. Spread butter evenly on bottom and up side of 9-inch pie plate. Press pecans, rounded side down, into butter. Pat brown sugar over pecans. Press dough in pie plate over brown sugar. Place apples in large bowl; sprinkle with lemon juice. Combine flour, granulated sugar, cinnamon, nutmeg and dash of salt in small bowl. Add to apples; toss. Turn into pie crust; spread evenly to keep top level. Roll out remaining dough on lightly floured surface to 1 inch larger than pie plate. Place over apples; fold edge under and flute. Cut slits for steam to escape. Bake 50 minutes. Remove from oven; cool 5 minutes. Invert onto serving plate.

Use your favorite pie crust recipe or see page 14.

Making Caramel Flowers

These caramel flowers are easy to make and add that special touch to any dessert. Place one fresh, soft caramel on a very lightly floured surface. Pressing down firmly, roll the caramel out to a 1-inch square. Roll the flattened caramel into a cone to resemble a flower.

"Just in Case" Pie

♦ Christa I. Schmitt from Sykesville, Maryland won first place in the Chocolate Baked Goods category in the Chocolate Recipe Contest sponsored by Lexington Market, Inc., Baltimore, Maryland.

Makes 6 to 8 servings

      Chocolate-Pecan Crust (recipe follows)
  1 envelope unflavored gelatin
  ¼ cup cold water
  1¾ cups whipping cream, divided
  1 cup semisweet chocolate chips
  2 eggs*
  1 teaspoon vanilla
  1 cup caramels (about 24)
  2 tablespoons butter or margarine
      Caramel flowers, for garnish

Prepare Chocolate-Pecan Crust; set aside. Sprinkle gelatin over water in small saucepan; let stand 1 minute. Stir over low heat until gelatin is completely dissolved, about 3 minutes. Stir in 1 cup of the cream. Heat just to a boil; immediately pour into a food processor or blender. Add chocolate chips and process until chocolate is completely melted, about 1 minute. Continue processing and add ½ cup of the cream, the eggs and vanilla. Pour into large bowl; refrigerate about 15 minutes or until thickened. Combine caramels, remaining ¼ cup of the cream and the butter in small saucepan. Simmer over low heat, stirring occasionally, until completely melted and smooth. Pour into prepared crust; let stand about 10 minutes. Beat thickened gelatin mixture until smooth. Pour over caramel layer; refrigerate 3 hours or until firm. Garnish with caramel flowers.

*Use clean, uncracked eggs.

Chocolate-Pecan Crust: Preheat oven to 350°F. Combine 2 cups chocolate wafer cookie crumbs, ¾ cup finely chopped pecans and ½ cup melted butter or margarine in small bowl. Press on bottom and up side of 9-inch deep-dish pie plate, forming a high rim. Bake 10 minutes. Cool completely before filling.

Mississippi Mist Pie

♦ Helen Peach from Meridian, Mississippi was the second place winner at the Dairylicious Pie Recipe Contest sponsored by the Southeast United Dairy Industry Association, Inc., Atlanta, Georgia.

Makes 6 to 8 servings

2 cups vanilla wafer crumbs (about 50 wafers)
5 tablespoons butter or margarine, melted
2 pints fresh strawberries
1 package (8 ounces) light cream cheese, softened
1 can (14 ounces) sweetened condensed milk
½ cup fresh lime juice (about 6 to 8 limes)
1 tablespoon green creme de menthe liqueur
1 cup whipping cream
3 tablespoons sugar
½ teaspoon vanilla
Lime slice, for garnish

Combine crumbs and butter in small bowl. Press firmly on bottom and up side of 9-inch pie plate. Refrigerate until firm.

Reserving 3 strawberries for garnish, cut off stem ends of remaining berries so they are no more than 1 inch tall. Arrange, cut ends down, on crust; refrigerate. Beat cream cheese until smooth. Add sweetened condensed milk; beat well. Add lime juice and liqueur; blend well. Pour into prepared crust, covering strawberries. Refrigerate at least one hour.

Whip cream until soft peaks form. Gradually add sugar and vanilla and whip until stiff and glossy. Using pastry bag with decorating tip, pipe lattice design on top of pie. Garnish with reserved strawberries and lime slice.

The secret to creating a superbly tender pie crust is to add a small amount of acid, such as lemon juice, vinegar, sour cream or even crème fraîche, to the pastry dough along with the liquid.

Nutty Chocolate Sour Cream Pie

♦ Sharon Roach from Lincoln, Illinois was a finalist in the Pies category of the Blue Ribbon Culinary Contest at the Illinois State Fair, Springfield, Illinois.

Makes 6 to 8 servings

   Flaky Pie Crust (recipe follows)
   4 eggs
   ⅔ cup packed brown sugar
   ⅔ cup sour cream
   ¼ cup honey
   1 teaspoon vanilla-nut flavoring
   ⅛ teaspoon salt
   2 cups chopped pecans
   1 cup semisweet chocolate chips

Prepare Flaky Pie Crust; set aside. Preheat oven to 350°F. Combine eggs, brown sugar, sour cream, honey, vanilla-nut flavoring and salt in large bowl; beat well. Stir in pecans and chocolate chips. Pour into prepared crust. Bake 40 to 45 minutes; cool completely on wire rack.

Flaky Pie Crust
   1 egg, beaten
   5 tablespoons cold water
   1 teaspoon vinegar
   1 teaspoon salt
   1 cup shortening
   3 cups all-purpose flour

Combine egg, water, vinegar and salt in medium bowl; set aside. Cut shortening into flour in large bowl until mixture resembles coarse crumbs. Add egg mixture; toss with fork until mixture holds together. Press together to form ball. Roll out on lightly floured surface to circle 1 inch larger than inverted 9-inch pie plate. Press in pie plate. Trim and flute edge.

DAYDREAM DESSERTS

Apple-Butter Pound Cake

♦ Helen Peach from Meridian, Mississippi was a grand prize winner in the Quaker® Corn Meal "Contemporary Classics" Recipe Contest.

Makes 10 to 12 servings

1½ cups granulated sugar
½ cup margarine, softened
1 package (8 ounces) cream cheese, softened
6 eggs
2 cups all-purpose flour
1 cup Quaker® Enriched Corn Meal
2 teaspoons baking powder
1 teaspoon ground cinnamon
¼ teaspoon salt (optional)
1 cup spiced apple butter
1 tablespoon bourbon (optional)
1 teaspoon vanilla
1 cup chopped pecans
   Creamy Glaze (recipe follows)

Preheat oven to 350°F. Grease 10-inch tube pan or 12-cup Bundt® pan. Beat sugar, margarine and cream cheese at high speed until light and fluffy. Add eggs, one at a time, mixing well after each addition. Combine flour, corn meal, baking powder, cinnamon and salt in small bowl. Add to sugar mixture alternately with combined apple butter, whiskey and vanilla. Mix at low speed until well blended. Stir in pecans. Spoon into prepared pan; spread evenly to edge. Bake 60 to 70 minutes or until wooden pick inserted into center comes out clean. Cool 10 minutes in pan; remove to wire rack. Cool completely. Drizzle with Creamy Glaze.

Creamy Glaze: Combine 1 cup powdered sugar, 4 to 5 teaspoons milk, 1½ teaspoons corn syrup and ¼ teaspoon vanilla or Bourbon whiskey in medium bowl; mix well.

Chocolate Chip & Mint Meringue Cookies

♦ Katherine Howell from Royal Oak, Michigan was a prize winner in the Cookies category at the Michigan State Fair, Detroit, Michigan.

Makes about 4 dozen cookies

  3 **egg whites**
  ½ **teaspoon cream of tartar**
    Pinch of salt
  ¾ **cup sugar**
  4 **drops green food coloring**
  4 **drops mint extract**
  1 **package (6 ounces) miniature chocolate chips**

Preheat oven to 375°F. Grease and lightly flour 2 cookie sheets. Beat egg whites with cream of tartar and salt until foamy. Gradually add sugar, 2 tablespoons at a time and beat until soft peaks form. Stir in food coloring and mint extract. Gently fold in chocolate chips. Drop by teaspoonfuls 1 inch apart onto prepared pans. Place in preheated oven, then turn off oven and let stand in oven with door closed 8 to 12 hours.

Carrot Cake

♦ Grace Meadows from Taylorville, Illinois was a finalist in the "Bake-A-Cake" category of the Blue Ribbon Culinary Contest at the Illinois State Fair, Springfield, Illinois.

Makes 8 to 10 servings

  4 **eggs**
1½ **cups vegetable oil**
  2 **cups all-purpose flour**
  2 **cups sugar**
  2 **teaspoons baking soda**
  2 **teaspoons baking powder**
  2 **teaspoons ground cinnamon**
  ¼ **teaspoon salt**
  3 **cups grated carrots**
1½ **cups coarsely chopped pecans or walnuts**
    Cream Cheese Icing (recipe follows)

Preheat oven to 350°F. Grease and flour 13 x 9-inch baking pan. Beat eggs and oil in small bowl. Combine flour, sugar, baking soda, baking powder, cinnamon and salt in large bowl. Add egg mixture; mix well. Stir in carrots and pecans. Pour into prepared pan. Bake 30 to 35 minutes or until wooden pick inserted into center comes out clean. Cool completely on wire rack. Spread with Cream Cheese Icing.

Cream Cheese Icing: Combine 1 box (16 ounces) powdered sugar, 1 package (8 ounces) cream cheese, softened, ½ cup margarine, softened and 1 teaspoon vanilla in medium bowl. Beat until smooth.

Spumoni is a Sicilian ice cream that is usually flavored with ground almonds and some type of fruit, such as cherries or lemons. It is lightened with whipped cream or egg whites and is a refreshing ending to a spicy Italian meal.

Simple Spumoni

♦ Jane Saribay from Pahala Elementary School in Pahala, Hawaii was a prize winner in a contest run by home economics teachers across the United States, sponsored by the Cherry Marketing Institute, Inc., Okemos, Michigan.

Makes about 1 quart

2 cups whipping cream
⅔ cup (7 ounces) sweetened condensed milk
½ teaspoon rum extract
1 can (21 ounces) cherry pie filling
½ cup chopped almonds
½ cup miniature chocolate chips

Combine cream, sweetened condensed milk and rum extract in large bowl; refrigerate 30 minutes. Remove from refrigerator and beat just until soft peaks form. Do not overbeat. Fold in cherry pie filling, almonds and chocolate chips. Transfer to 8 × 8-inch pan. Cover and freeze about 4 hours or until firm. Scoop out to serve. Garnish as desired.

Chocolate Chip Cake

♦ Darren Roach from Lincoln, Illinois was a finalist in the "Bake-A-Cake" category of the Blue Ribbon Culinary Contest at the Illinois State Fair, Springfield, Illinois.

Makes 8 to 10 servings

  2 cups all-purpose flour
  1 cup packed dark brown sugar
  ½ cup granulated sugar
  1 tablespoon baking powder
  1 teaspoon salt
  ½ teaspoon baking soda
  ½ cup shortening
1¼ cups milk
  3 eggs
  ½ cup semisweet chocolate chips, finely chopped
1½ teaspoons vanilla
  ¼ cup finely chopped walnuts
    Butterscotch Filling (recipe follows)
    Chocolate Chip Glaze (recipe follows)

Preheat oven to 350°F. Grease and flour two 9-inch round baking pans. Combine all ingredients except walnuts, Butterscotch Filling and Chocolate Glaze in large bowl, mixing at low speed 30 seconds and scraping bowl constantly. Beat at high speed 3 minutes, scraping bowl occasionally. Pour into prepared pans. Bake 40 to 45 minutes or until wooden pick inserted into center comes out clean. Cool completely on wire rack.

Spread 1 cake layer with Butterscotch Filling; sprinkle with walnuts. Top with second cake layer and pour Chocolate Chip Glaze over top of cake. Garnish with additional walnuts if desired.

Butterscotch Filling: Combine ½ cup packed light brown sugar, ¼ cup cornstarch and ¼ teaspoon salt in medium saucepan. Add ½ cup water; cook over medium heat until mixture comes to a boil, stirring constantly. Boil and stir 1 minute. Stir in 1 tablespoon butter; cool.

Chocolate Chip Glaze: Combine ½ cup semisweet chocolate chips, 2 tablespoons butter and 1 tablespoon light corn syrup in small saucepan. Cook over low heat until chocolate melts, stirring constantly. Cool slightly.

When it first started in 1954, the Black Walnut Baking Contest was a regional competition for the best recipes in eight counties of West Virginia. The county winners were then invited to prepare their dishes during a bake-off at the annual Black Walnut Festival. The popularity of the contest has now expanded into a major statewide competition.

Black Walnut Fudge

♦ Una Belle Waskey from Sandyville, West Virginia was the third place winner in the Black Walnut Bake-Off at the Black Walnut Festival, Spencer, West Virginia.

Makes about 3 pounds

4 cups sugar
½ cup margarine
1 can (12 ounces) evaporated milk
3 tablespoons light corn syrup
1 pound white chocolate-flavored chips*
1 jar (13 ounces) marshmallow creme
1 cup chopped black walnuts
1 tablespoon vanilla

Grease 13 × 9-inch pan. Combine sugar, margarine, evaporated milk and corn syrup in large saucepan. Cook over medium heat, stirring until sugar dissolves. Stop stirring and continue heating until mixture reaches soft-ball stage (234°F) on candy thermometer. Remove from heat and stir in white chocolate chips until melted; add marshmallow creme, walnuts and vanilla, beating well after each addition. Pour into prepared pan. Cool completely. Cut into squares.

*Do not use confectioner's coating or compound chocolate.

ong, long ago, a proper pound cake was made from a pound of butter, a pound of flour, a pound of eggs and a pound of sugar. Modern cooks have modified this formula. Today, all the same ingredients are used, but the proportions have changed considerably. While pound cake cannot be classified as a health food, a well-made one is a comforting thing to have, especially when it is toasted and topped with black cherry preserves.

Sour Cream Pound Cake

♦ Jeanette Martin from Jacksonville, Illinois was a finalist in the "Bake-A-Cake" category of the Blue Ribbon Culinary Contest at the Illinois State Fair, Springfield, Illinois.

Makes 10 to 12 servings

1 cup butter, softened
2¾ cups sugar
1 tablespoon vanilla
2 teaspoons grated orange peel
6 eggs
3 cups all-purpose flour
½ teaspoon salt
¼ teaspoon baking soda
1 cup sour cream
Citrus Topping (recipe follows)

Preheat oven to 325°F. Grease 10-inch tube pan. Beat butter in large bowl until creamy; gradually add sugar, beating until light and fluffy. Beat in vanilla and orange peel. Add eggs, one at a time, beating 1 minute after each addition. Combine flour, salt and baking soda in small bowl. Add to butter mixture alternately with sour cream beginning and ending with flour mixture. Pour into prepared pan. Bake 1 hour and 15 minutes or until wooden pick inserted into center comes out clean. Spoon Citrus Topping over hot cake; cool in pan 15 minutes. Remove from pan to wire rack; cool completely.

Citrus Topping

⅓ cup slivered orange peel
2 teaspoons salt
⅓ cup orange juice
½ cup sugar, divided
⅓ cup lemon juice
1 teaspoon vanilla

Combine orange peel and salt in medium saucepan. Add enough water to cover; boil 2 minutes. Drain. Add orange juice and ¼ cup of the sugar; simmer 10 minutes. Add remaining ¼ cup sugar, the lemon juice and vanilla; stir until smooth.

Apricot Squares

♦ Alma Lauer from Abilene, Kansas was the first place winner in the Cookie category in the annual recipe contest sponsored by the *Reflector-Chronicle*, Abilene, Kansas.

Makes about 2 dozen squares

  1 cup butter, softened
  ½ cup granulated sugar
  ½ teaspoon vanilla
  2 cups all-purpose flour
  1 jar (12 ounces) apricot jam
  2 egg whites
  ½ teaspoon almond extract
  1 cup powdered sugar
  ½ cup slivered almonds

Preheat oven to 350°F. Cream butter, granulated sugar and vanilla in large bowl until fluffy. Stir in flour; blend well. Spread in ungreased 13 × 9-inch baking pan. Bake 15 minutes. Cool completely on wire rack.

Spread jam over cooled crust. Beat egg whites and almond extract in medium bowl until soft peaks form. Gradually add powdered sugar and beat until stiff and glossy. Spread mixture over jam. Sprinkle with almonds. Bake at 350°F 15 to 20 minutes. Cool completely on wire rack. Cut into 2-inch squares.

GLORIOUS CHOCOLATE

Grand Marnier is one of the most popular orange-flavored liqueurs and is widely enjoyed in America. It comes from an infusion of the finest cognac with the peels of luscious Curaçao oranges. Some other orange-flavored liqueurs include Triple Sec, Cointreau and Curaçao.

Grand Marnier Brownies

♦ Mary P. Murphy from Hampton, New Hampshire was the first place winner in the Topsfield Fair Baking Competition sponsored by the Essex Agricultural Society, Topsfield, Massachusetts.

Makes about 2 dozen brownies

    2 squares (1 ounce each) unsweetened chocolate
    2 cups sugar
    ½ cup vegetable oil
    ½ cup Grand Marnier liqueur or other
        orange-flavored liqueur
    ¼ cup chocolate-flavored syrup
    4 eggs, beaten
    3 tablespoons unsweetened cocoa
    2 teaspoons grated orange peel
    1 teaspoon orange juice
 1¼ cups all-purpose flour
    1 teaspoon baking powder
    1 package (12 ounces) semisweet chocolate chips,
        divided
    2 tablespoons shortening
      Orange peel strips, for garnish

Preheat oven to 350°F. Grease 13 × 9-inch pan. Melt unsweetened chocolate in top of double boiler over hot, not boiling, water. Remove from heat and mix in sugar, oil, liqueur, syrup, eggs, cocoa, orange peel and juice. Stir in flour, baking powder and 1⅓ cups of the chocolate chips. Spread batter evenly in prepared pan. Bake 22 minutes; do not overbake.

As soon as brownies are removed from oven, melt remaining ⅔ cup chocolate chips and shortening in top of double boiler over hot, not boiling water; stir until smooth. Spread hot chocolate mixture over warm brownies. Cool completely in pan on wire rack. Cut into 2-inch squares. Garnish with orange peel strips if desired.

Frozen Chocolate Cheesecake

♦ Sandy Johnson from Fort Myers, Florida was the first prize winner in the Chocolate Festival Recipe Contest, sponsored by The Kidney Foundation at the Sheraton Harbor Place, Fort Myers, Florida.

Makes about 8 servings

1½ **cups chocolate or vanilla wafer cookie crumbs**
 ⅓ **cup margarine, melted**
 1 **package (8 ounces) cream cheese, softened**
 ½ **cup sugar, divided**
 2 **eggs,* separated**
 1 **cup semisweet chocolate chips, melted**
 1 **teaspoon vanilla**
 1 **cup whipping cream, lightly whipped**
 ¾ **cup chopped pecans**
   Chocolate curls,** for garnish

Preheat oven to 325°F. Combine crumbs and margarine; press on bottom and up side of 9-inch pie plate. Bake 10 minutes. Cool completely on wire rack.

Beat cream cheese with ¼ cup of the sugar in large bowl. Beat egg yolks; gradually stir into cheese mixture with melted chocolate chips and vanilla. Beat egg whites in small bowl until foamy. Gradually add remaining ¼ cup sugar, beating until soft peaks form. Gently fold egg whites into chocolate mixture. Fold in whipped cream and pecans. Pour chocolate filling into prepared crust and freeze until firm. Garnish with chocolate curls.

*Use clean, uncracked eggs.
**See tip on page 6 for making chocolate curls.

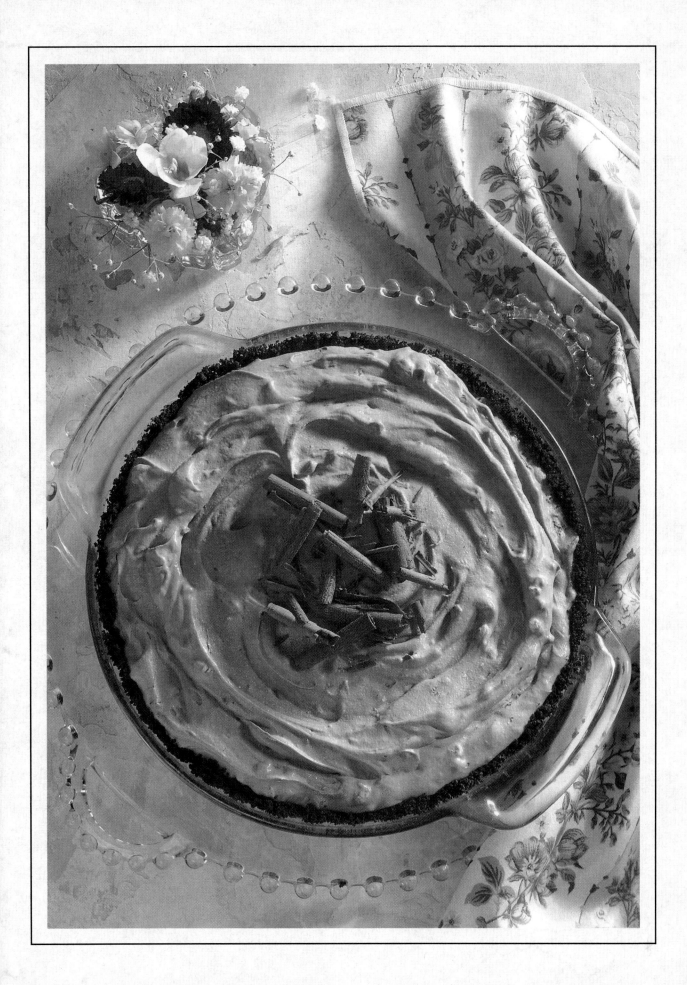

Unsweetened cocoa is formed by extracting most of the cocoa butter from pure chocolate and grinding the remaining chocolate solids into a powder. "Dutch process" cocoa is unsweetened cocoa that has been treated with an alkali, giving it a darker appearance and a slightly less bitter flavor. In recipes, do not substitute sweetened cocoa, the type that is used for making hot chocolate, for unsweetened cocoa.

Chocolate Almond Ladyfinger Crown

♦ Jill Earl from Baltimore, Maryland won second place in the Chocolate Specialties category of the Chocolate Recipe Contest sponsored by Lexington Market, Inc., Baltimore, Maryland.

Makes about 12 servings

  2 envelopes unflavored gelatin
1¼ cups sugar, divided
  ¾ cup unsweetened cocoa
  4 eggs,* separated
2¼ cups milk
  ⅓ cup almond-flavored liqueur
  2 packages (3 ounces each) ladyfingers, split
1½ cups whipping cream, whipped
     Almond Cream (recipe follows)
     Sliced almonds, for garnish

Mix gelatin with 1 cup of the sugar and the cocoa in medium saucepan. Blend in egg yolks beaten with milk and let stand 1 minute. Stir over low heat until gelatin is completely dissolved, about 5 minutes. Using a wire whisk, beat until completely blended, then stir in liqueur. Pour into large bowl and refrigerate, stirring occasionally, until mixture mounds slightly when dropped from spoon. Meanwhile, line bottom and side of 9-inch springform pan with ladyfingers; refrigerate.

Beat egg whites in large bowl until soft peaks form. Gradually add remaining ¼ cup sugar and beat until stiff and glossy. Fold egg whites into gelatin mixture, then fold in whipped cream. Pour mixture into prepared pan and refrigerate until firm. To serve, remove side of pan. Garnish with Almond Cream and sliced almonds.

Almond Cream: Beat ½ cup whipping cream with 1 tablespoon powdered sugar in small bowl until stiff and glossy. Fold in 1 tablespoon almond-flavored liqueur.

*Use clean, uncracked eggs.

Mousse is a French word meaning froth or foam. It can be sweet or savory, but is always light and airy due to the addition of beaten egg whites and/or cream. When most people think of a mousse, they think of chocolate. Not so long ago chocolate mousse was on almost every menu and most accomplished cooks had at least two recipes for it. Like all the best desserts, it is made with eggs, sugar, cream and, of course, chocolate.

Chocolate Mousse Pie

♦ Terri Kaiser from West Haven, Connecticut was the first place winner in the No-Bake category in the Pie Contest, sponsored by *The Hartford Courant*, Hartford, Connecticut.

Makes 10 servings

  1 package (8½ ounces) chocolate wafer cookies, finely crushed
  ½ cup butter, melted
  16 ounces semisweet chocolate chips (about 2⅔ cups)
  6 eggs,* separated
  2 eggs,* whole
  5 cups whipping cream, divided
  ⅓ cup plus ¼ cup powdered sugar, divided
  2 teaspoons vanilla, divided
  ¼ cup miniature chocolate chips
    Fresh raspberries and mint leaves, for garnish

Combine crumbs and butter in medium bowl. Press on bottom and up side of 9-inch springform pan; set aside.

Melt chocolate chips in top of double boiler over hot, not boiling, water. Beat egg yolks with the 2 whole eggs. Add to hot melted chocolate; mix well. Beat egg whites in large bowl until stiff peaks form; set aside. Whip 3 cups of the cream in large bowl until soft peaks form. Gradually add ⅓ cup of the sugar and 1 teaspoon of the vanilla; whip until stiff and glossy. Fold chocolate mixture into whipped cream. Fold beaten egg whites and ¼ cup miniature chocolate chips into cream mixture. Pour into prepared crust and refrigerate at least 3 hours. (Pour any extra filling into individual dishes.)

Whip remaining 2 cups cream in large bowl until soft peaks form. Gradually add remaining ¼ cup sugar and 1 teaspoon vanilla. Spread over chilled pie. To serve, remove side of pan and garnish with raspberries and mint leaves.

Use clean, uncracked eggs.

Not really chocolate at all because it lacks chocolate liquor (the main component in unsweetened chocolate), white chocolate is cocoa butter with added sugar, milk and flavorings (often vanilla or vanillin). It is more delicate than other chocolates and burns easily. So melt it carefully using a double boiler and stirring constantly.

To make white chocolate triangles, spread melted white chocolate into a rectangle on a waxed paper-lined baking sheet. Refrigerate until set but not hard. With tip of a knife make a diagonal score cutting rectangle into two triangles. Refrigerate until firm.

Chocolate Bombe

♦ Pat Miceli from Baltimore, Maryland won third place in the Chocolate Recipe Contest sponsored by Lexington Market, Inc., Baltimore, Maryland.

Makes about 8 servings

1 package (12 ounces) semisweet chocolate chips
5 whole eggs,* divided
3 egg whites,*
1¼ cups sugar, divided
1 cup flour
1 teaspoon baking soda
1 cup unsweetened cocoa
1 cup water
¼ cup vegetable oil
   Melted white chocolate, for garnish

Melt chocolate chips in top of double boiler over hot, not boiling, water. Beat 3 of the whole eggs and add to chocolate. Continue to cook, stirring constantly, until mixture starts to bubble and thicken. Beat 3 egg whites in large bowl until soft peaks form. Gradually add ¼ cup of the sugar and beat until stiff and glossy. Fold whites into chocolate mixture. Pour into oiled 2- to 3-quart mold or bowl; cover and refrigerate 4 hours.

Preheat oven to 375°F. Grease and flour 8- or 9-inch round baking pan. Sift flour with baking soda. Beat the remaining 2 whole eggs and 1 cup sugar in medium bowl until creamy. Stir in cocoa and flour mixture. Add water and oil; mix until smooth. Pour batter into prepared pan. Bake 18 to 20 minutes or until wooden pick inserted into center comes out clean. Cool 10 minutes in pan. Loosen edge and remove to wire rack; cool completely.

Unmold mousse onto cake. Cover with plastic wrap and refrigerate at least 4 hours. Drizzle with melted white chocolate before serving.

*Use clean, uncracked eggs.

Chocolate, and related candies and baked goods, is a 5 billion dollar industry. Last year the average American ate about 11 pounds of chocolate. Milk chocolate is still the most popular but semisweet has a loyal following.

Chocolate Rice Pudding

♦ Teresa Hubbard from Russelville, Alabama won first prize in the Dessert category of *Essence*/Uncle Ben's® Good Eating Recipe Contest.

Makes 6 servings

1 cup uncooked Uncle Ben's® Converted® Brand Rice
¼ cup sugar
2 teaspoons cornstarch
2 cups milk
½ teaspoon vanilla
2 egg yolks, beaten
½ cup semisweet chocolate chips
Whipped cream and cookies for serving

Cook rice according to package directions in large saucepan. Combine sugar and cornstarch; add to hot rice in saucepan. Stir in milk. Bring to a boil, stirring occasionally. Boil 1 minute, stirring constantly. Remove from heat; stir in vanilla. Stir about 1 cup of hot rice mixture into beaten egg yolks in small bowl. Stir back into remaining rice mixture in saucepan. Cook over medium heat, stirring frequently, just until mixture starts to bubble. Remove from heat; add chocolate chips and stir until melted. Spoon into individual serving dishes. Chill. Serve with whipped cream and cookies if desired.

See Dessert Basics on pages 4 and 5 for tips on beating egg whites.

Soufflé Making Tips

To ensure perfect soufflés, start by choosing the right dish. Choose a porcelain or ceramic dish with straight sides made just for soufflés. To extend the side and support the soufflé use a waxed paper "collar." Fold a sheet of waxed paper in half lengthwise and carefully tape it to the dish, overlapping ends.

See Dessert Basics on pages 4 and 5 for tips on beating egg whites.

Gently fold beaten egg whites into soufflé mixture just until combined. Too much agitation can cause the egg whites to break down and the soufflé to fall.

Black Forest Soufflé

♦ Angie Leialoha Oliveros from Pahala, Hawaii was a prize winner in a contest run by home economics teachers across the United States sponsored by the Cherry Marketing Institute, Inc., Okemos, Michigan.

Makes about 10 servings

    3 eggs,* separated
    2 cups milk
    2 envelopes unflavored gelatin
    ¾ cup sugar, divided
    4 squares (1 ounce each) semisweet chocolate
    2 teaspoons rum extract
 1½ teaspoons vanilla
    2 cups whipping cream, divided
    1 can (21 ounces) cherry pie filling
    ⅓ cup chopped almonds
      Maraschino cherries and chocolate curls,**
        for garnish

Tape a 3-inch-wide greased and floured waxed paper or parchment paper "collar" around rim of 1-quart soufflé dish, greased side in. Beat egg yolks and milk in small bowl. Mix gelatin with ½ cup of the sugar in medium saucepan. Add egg mixture; let stand 1 minute. Stir over low heat until gelatin is completely dissolved, about 5 minutes. Add chocolate; stir constantly until melted. Beat until thoroughly blended. Stir in rum extract and vanilla. Pour into large bowl and refrigerate, stirring occasionally, until mixture mounds slightly when dropped from spoon.

Beat egg whites in large bowl until soft peaks form. Gradually add remaining ¼ cup sugar and beat until stiff and glossy. Fold into gelatin mixture. Whip 1½ cups of the cream in medium bowl until stiff peaks form; fold into gelatin mixture. Fold in cherry pie filling and almonds. Pour mixture into prepared dish and refrigerate until set. To serve, whip remaining ½ cup cream until stiff peaks form. Remove collar and decorate with whipped cream, maraschino cherries and chocolate curls.

*Use clean, uncracked eggs.
**See tip on page 6 for making chocolate curls.

Chocolate Chiffon Cake

♦ Jeanette Monahan from Albuquerque, New Mexico was a finalist in the Cakes category at the New Mexico State Fair, Albuquerque, New Mexico.

Makes about 12 servings

1 bar (4 ounces) sweet baking chocolate
½ cup hot water
5 eggs, separated
⅔ cup sugar
1 cup all-purpose flour
1 teaspoon baking powder
½ teaspoon salt
1 teaspoon vanilla
Powdered sugar

Preheat oven to 350°F. Melt chocolate in hot water; set aside. Beat egg whites in large bowl until soft peaks form. Gradually add sugar and beat until stiff and glossy; set aside. Combine melted chocolate mixture, egg yolks, flour, baking powder, salt and vanilla in small bowl; beat 1 minute with electric mixer. Carefully fold chocolate mixture into egg whites until blended. Pour into ungreased 10-inch tube pan. Bake 45 to 50 minutes or until top springs back when lightly touched. Invert in pan; cool completely. Remove from pan; sprinkle with powdered sugar.

FRUIT FANTASIES

Fruit Salsa Sundaes

♦ Charlene Margesson was the Grand Prize winner in the "Skinny Dip" Recipe Contest, sponsored by Dreyer's/Edy's Grand Light®.

Makes 4 servings

   4 (6-inch) flour tortillas
1½ cups diced peeled peaches
1½ cups diced strawberries
   2 tablespoons sugar
   1 tablespoon finely chopped crystallized ginger
   ½ teaspoon grated lime peel
   4 scoops (4 ounces each) Dreyer's/Edy's Grand
      Light® Vanilla
   Sprigs of fresh mint, for garnish

Preheat oven to 350°F. Soften tortillas according to package directions. Press each one down in ungreased 10-ounce custard cup. Bake 10 to 15 minutes or until crisp. Set aside to cool.

Combine peaches, strawberries, sugar, ginger and lime peel in large bowl; mix gently until well blended. To assemble, remove tortillas from custard cups. Place each tortilla shell on dessert plate and fill with 1 scoop of Grand Light®. Spoon equal portions of fruit salsa over tops. Garnish with mint sprigs.

Cobblers, pandowdies, buckles, grunts and slumps are all old-fashioned fruit desserts that have lost none of their charm with the passing of generations. The fruit can be anything from huckleberries and blueberries to apples and peaches. Cobblers are usually baked in a deep dish and often have a pastry crust and/or a biscuit-like topping. This version has a crunchy brown sugar and oatmeal topping.

Crunch Peach Cobbler

♦ Gladys Montgomery from Orangevale, California was a prize winner in the Peach Cobbler Contest at the California State Fair.

Makes about 6 servings

1 can (29 ounces) *or* 2 cans (16 ounces each) cling peach slices in syrup
⅓ cup plus 1 tablespoon granulated sugar, divided
1 tablespoon cornstarch
½ teaspoon vanilla
½ cup packed brown sugar
2 cups all-purpose flour, divided
⅓ cup uncooked rolled oats
¼ cup margarine or butter, melted
½ teaspoon ground cinnamon
½ teaspoon salt
½ cup shortening
4 to 5 tablespoons cold water
Whipped cream, for serving

Drain peach slices, reserving ¾ cup syrup. Combine ⅓ cup of the granulated sugar and the cornstarch in small saucepan. Slowly add reserved peach liquid, stirring to make sauce smooth; add vanilla. Cook over low heat, stirring constantly, until thickened. Set aside.

Combine brown sugar, ½ cup of the flour, the oats, margarine and cinnamon in small bowl; stir until crumbly. Set aside.

Preheat oven to 350°F. Combine remaining 1½ cups flour, 1 tablespoon granulated sugar and the salt in small bowl. Cut in shortening until mixture resembles coarse crumbs. Sprinkle water, 1 tablespoon at a time, over flour mixture and toss lightly until mixture holds together. Press together to form ball. Roll out on floured surface to 10-inch square. Press on bottom and about 1 inch up sides of 8 × 8-inch baking dish.

Layer peaches, sauce and crumb topping over crust. Bake 45 minutes. Serve warm or at room temperature with whipped cream.

Fabulous Fruit-Cheese Tart

♦ Jean S. Cooper from Falls Church, Virginia won second prize in the Polly-O® International Recipe Competition sponsored by Pollio Dairy Products Corporation.

Makes 6 servings

- **1 cup all-purpose flour**
- **½ cup plus 3 tablespoons sugar, divided**
- **6 tablespoons cold butter**
- **1 egg yolk**
- **3 tablespoons water, divided**
- **½ teaspoon almond extract**
- **Pinch salt**
- **½ cup apple or currant jelly**
- **1 pound Polly-O® ricotta cheese**
- **1 package (3 ounces) cream cheese, softened**
- **3 tablespoons orange-flavored liqueur**
- **1 pint strawberries, hulled and cut in half**
- **2 firm kiwifruit, peeled and sliced**

Combine flour and 3 tablespoons of the sugar in large bowl. Cut in butter until mixture resembles coarse crumbs. Add egg yolk, 1 tablespoon of the water, the almond extract and salt; toss with fork until mixture holds together. Press together to form ball. Refrigerate 30 minutes.

Preheat oven to 400°F. Roll out dough on floured surface to circle 1 inch larger than inverted 9-inch tart pan. Press into tart pan; trim edge. Prick dough and line with foil. Fill with dried beans, uncooked rice or pie weights. Bake 12 to 14 minutes. Remove foil lining and beans. Cool completely on wire rack.

Melt jelly and remaining 2 tablespoons water in small saucepan, stirring constantly. Brush on cooled crust. Combine ricotta cheese, cream cheese, remaining ½ cup sugar and the liqueur; beat until smooth. Spread in glazed tart shell. Arrange strawberry halves and kiwi slices in circles on top of tart. Refrigerate before serving.

A maretti cookies are Italian meringue cookies and can be purchased at Italian or specialty food shops. If desired, substitute an equal amount of finely chopped toasted hazelnuts or almonds.

The Golden Strawberry

♦ Kevin P. Dunn from Allegan, Michigan was a prize winner in the Knox® Unflavored Gelatine Recipe Contest, sponsored by Thomas J. Lipton, Inc., at The Culinary Institute of America, Hyde Park, New York.

Makes about 8 servings

- 1 envelope Knox® Unflavored Gelatine
- ⅓ cup strawberry-flavored liqueur
- 6 ounces Montrachet goat cheese*
- 4 tablespoons sugar, divided
- ¼ cup sour cream
- 2 tablespoons honey
- ½ teaspoon ground cinnamon
- ¼ teaspoon ground nutmeg
- 3 egg whites**
- ½ cup whipping cream, whipped
- 1 pint strawberries, quartered
- 6 ounces amaretti cookies, coarsely crushed (about 1 cup)
- Whipped cream, additional strawberries and amaretti cookies, for garnish

Sprinkle gelatine over liqueur in small saucepan; let stand 1 minute. Stir over low heat until gelatine is completely dissolved, about 5 minutes. Using a wire whisk, blend in cheese and 2 tablespoons of the sugar; pour into large bowl. Blend in sour cream, honey, cinnamon and nutmeg; set aside.

Beat egg whites in medium bowl until soft peaks form. Gradually add remaining 2 tablespoons sugar and beat until stiff and glossy. Fold egg whites into gelatine mixture, then fold in whipped cream and quartered strawberries. Alternately layer strawberry mixture with crushed cookies in parfait glasses or dessert dishes; refrigerate until completely set. Garnish with additional whipped cream, strawberries and cookies.

*Montrachet cheese is a white chèvre from the Burgundy region of France. It has a soft, moist and creamy texture and a mildly tangy flavor. It can be found in the gourmet or imported cheese section of most supermarkets or specialty food stores.

**Use clean, uncracked eggs.

Apricot Roll-Ups

♦ Harriet Kuhn from Patterson, California was the
Apricot Sweepstakes winner at the Patterson Apricot
Fiesta, sponsored by the Apricot Advisory Board,
Walnut Creek, California.

Makes 20 to 26 roll-ups

    4 cups dried apricots
    1 can (12 ounces) apricot-pineapple nectar
 1½ cups water
    ½ cup sugar
    2 tablespoons lemon juice
    1 tablespoon quick-cooking tapioca
    2 cups finely chopped walnuts
    1 package (7 ounces) shredded coconut
    1 package egg roll wrappers
      Vegetable oil, for frying
      Sour cream and chocolate sauce, for dipping

Combine apricots, nectar, water, sugar and lemon
juice in large saucepan; bring to a boil. Remove
from heat; cover and let stand 1 hour. Drain,
reserving liquid. Finely chop apricots. Combine
apricots, reserved liquid and tapioca in same
saucepan; bring to a boil, stirring constantly.
Remove from heat and let stand 20 minutes. Stir in
walnuts and coconut.

For each roll-up, place about 2 heaping tablespoons
of the apricot mixture on lower half of egg roll
wrapper. Moisten left and right edges with water.
Fold bottom edge up to just cover filling. Fold left
and right edges ½ inch over; roll up jelly-roll
fashion. Moisten top edge and seal.

Heat about 2 inches oil in heavy skillet to 370°F.
Fry roll-ups, a few at a time, seam side down in hot
oil until golden brown; turn as necessary. Drain on
paper towels. Serve with bowls of sour cream and
chocolate sauce for dipping.

The marvelous macadamia nut is second-to-none for its buttery-smooth flavor and delectable crunch. It is the world's most expensive nut and considered by many to also be the world's finest. Native to Australia, the macadamia tree was named after the man who cultivated it, chemist John MacAdam. It was brought to Hawaii in the late nineteenth century and has since become the state's third largest crop.

Pineapple Macadamia Cheesepie

♦ Joan Simon was the grand prize winner in the Dessert category in "Generations of Good Cooking," an employee contest sponsored by Dole® Packaged Foods Company.

Makes 6 servings

CRUST
  1 cup chopped macadamia nuts
  ¾ cup graham cracker crumbs
  6 tablespoons butter, melted
  2 tablespoons sugar

FILLING
  12 ounces cream cheese, softened
  1 egg
  ¾ cup plain yogurt
  ½ cup sugar
  1 teaspoon vanilla
  1 can (8 ounces) Dole® Crushed Pineapple
      in Juice

To make crust, combine nuts, crumbs, butter and 2 tablespoons sugar in small bowl. Press on bottom and up side of 8- or 9-inch pie plate; refrigerate until firm.

Preheat oven to 350°F. Combine cream cheese, egg, yogurt, ½ cup sugar and vanilla in medium bowl; blend thoroughly. Drain pineapple, pressing out excess juice with back of spoon. Spread all but 2 tablespoons of pineapple over prepared crust. Pour cheese filling over pineapple. Bake 20 minutes; cool completely on wire rack. Refrigerate at least 2 hours. Before serving, garnish with reserved 2 tablespoons pineapple and additional macadamia nuts.

Acini di Pepe Fruit Pudding

♦ Verda Seeklander from Hazelton, North Dakota was the second place winner in the Delicious Desserts category of the Pasta Contest sponsored by the North Dakota Wheat Commission.

Makes 8 servings

> 1 cup acini di pepe or other small pasta, cooked and drained
> ¾ cup milk
> 1 can (20 ounces) crushed pineapple in juice, drained, reserving ½ cup juice
> 2 eggs, well beaten
> ½ cup granulated sugar
> ½ teaspoon grated lemon peel
> ½ teaspoon ground cinnamon (optional)
> ⅔ cup packed brown sugar
> ⅔ cup finely chopped walnuts
> ¼ cup all-purpose flour
> 6 tablespoons butter or margarine
> Whipped topping, for serving

Cook acini di pepe according to package directions; drain well. Preheat oven to 375°F. Grease 8 × 8-inch baking pan. Combine pasta, milk, reserved ½ cup pineapple juice, the eggs, granulated sugar, lemon peel and cinnamon in large bowl. Spoon mixture into prepared pan. Top with pineapple.

Combine brown sugar, walnuts and flour in small bowl; cut in butter until mixture resembles coarse crumbs. Sprinkle over pineapple. Bake 60 minutes or until knife inserted into center comes out clean. Serve warm or cold with whipped topping.

Note: Any type of fruit canned in fruit juice may be used, such as fruit cocktail, peaches, pears, etc.

*B*ees have been
producing honey for more
than 5 million years, and
it has been harvested for
almost 3 million. A
worker bee will toil for
an entire lifetime to make
¹⁄₁₂ teaspoon of honey
(about 3 drops). Darker
honeys are stronger in
flavor than lighter
honeys.

Apples 'n' Honey Nut Tart

♦ Mary King of Concordia, Kansas was a grand prize winner in the Dessert category of the "Celebrate! Kansas Food" Recipe Contest.

Makes 8 to 10 servings

1¼ cups all-purpose flour
⅓ cup wheat germ
⅓ cup packed brown sugar
½ teaspoon salt
¾ teaspoon grated orange peel, divided
½ cup cold butter, cut into pieces
1 egg, beaten
1 cup pecans, coarsely chopped
⅓ cup golden raisins
8 tablespoons honey, divided
2 tablespoons butter, melted
½ teaspoon ground cinnamon
4 cups peeled, cored, ¼-inch-thick apple slices
⅓ cup orange marmalade
⅔ cup whipping cream

Combine flour, wheat germ, sugar, salt and ½ teaspoon of the orange peel in large bowl. Cut in ½ cup cold butter until mixture resembles coarse crumbs. Stir in egg until well blended; press in bottom and up side of 9-inch tart pan with removable bottom. Freeze until very firm, about 30 minutes.

Preheat oven to 350°F. Sprinkle pecans and raisins on chilled crust. Combine 6 tablespoons of the honey, the 2 tablespoons melted butter, remaining ¼ teaspoon orange peel, the cinnamon and apple slices in large bowl; stir to coat apples. Arrange apple slices in circular pattern on top of pecans and raisins. Drizzle any honey mixture left in bowl over apples. Bake 50 to 55 minutes or until apples are tender. Heat marmalade until warm; brush over apples. Cool; remove side of tart pan. Whip cream until soft peaks form. Add remaining 2 tablespoons honey and whip until stiff and glossy. Serve with tart.

Note: If desired, sprinkle 1 cup granola over top of tart after it has been glazed with marmalade.

Raspberry Cheesecake Blossoms

♦ Vienna Taylor from Richmond, Virginia was a finalist in the Dairy Dessert Recipe Contest, sponsored by the Southeast United Dairy Industry Association, Atlanta, Georgia.

Makes 12 servings

> 8 sheets phyllo dough
> ¼ cup butter, melted
> ½ cup cottage cheese
> 1 package (8 ounces) cream cheese, softened
> 1 egg
> ½ cup plus 3 tablespoons sugar, divided
> 4 teaspoons lemon juice, divided
> ½ teaspoon vanilla
> 3 packages (10 ounces each) frozen raspberries, thawed and drained, reserving syrup
> Fresh raspberries and sliced kiwifruit, for garnish

Preheat oven to 350°F. Grease 12 (2½-inch) muffin cups. Layer 4 sheets of phyllo dough on waxed paper, brushing each sheet with melted butter. Repeat with remaining 4 sheets, forming separate stack. Cut each stack in half lengthwise and then in thirds crosswise, to make a total of 12 squares. Gently fit each stacked square into prepared muffin cup, forming 4-petaled blossom.

Process the cheeses, egg, 3 tablespoons of the sugar, 1 teaspoon of the lemon juice and the vanilla in a food processor or blender until smooth. Divide evenly among blossom cups. Bake 10 to 15 minutes or until lightly browned. Carefully remove from muffin cups to cool.

Bring reserved raspberry syrup to a boil in small saucepan. Cook until reduced to ¾ cup, stirring occasionally. Purée thawed raspberries in food processor or blender; press through sieve to remove seeds. Combine raspberry purée, syrup, remaining ½ cup sugar and 3 teaspoons lemon juice. Refrigerate.

To serve, spoon raspberry sauce onto 12 dessert plates. Place cheesecake blossom on each plate. Top with fresh raspberries and arrange kiwifruit in sauce to resemble leaves.

There are two very different fruits that share the name of currant. The first, most often used in baking and called for in this recipe, is a tiny, dark dried Zante grape. Originally from Corinth, Greece it is now available year-round in most stores. Raisins and currants may be used interchangeably in recipes. The second variety is a tiny berry related to the gooseberry. It comes in black, red and white varieties and is used in preserves and jellies, liqueurs and pie fillings.

Meringue Apples

♦ Janet Langhart was the American Regional Cuisine Award winner at the March of Dimes Gourmet Gala in Boston, Massachusetts.

Makes 6 servings

6 large baking apples (preferably Cortlands)
½ cup packed brown sugar
⅓ cup currants
3 tablespoons honey
3 tablespoons butter, melted
3 tablespoons rum
1 tablespoon grated fresh ginger
½ teaspoon ground cinnamon
½ teaspoon ground nutmeg
¼ teaspoon ground mace
4 egg whites*
¾ cup granulated sugar
  Finely grated peel of 2 lemons (about
    2 tablespoons)

Preheat oven to 350°F. Core apples. With vegetable peeler, cut away 1 inch of peel from top of each apple. Scoop out some of apple around top. Arrange apples upright in 13 x 9-inch baking dish. Mix brown sugar, currants, honey, butter, rum, ginger, cinnamon, nutmeg and mace in small bowl. Fill each apple cavity with mixture; distribute any remaining mixture around apples in dish. Pour about 1 inch water into dish. Bake 40 minutes or until apples are tender, but not falling apart; remove from oven. *Increase oven temperature to 450°F.*

Beat egg whites in large bowl until soft peaks form. Gradually add granulated sugar, 1 tablespoon at a time, beating until stiff and glossy. Fold in grated lemon peel. Pipe or spoon meringue decoratively on top of each apple. Return apples to oven and bake about 5 minutes or until meringue is golden. (Watch carefully so meringue does not burn.) Serve hot or at room temperature. Garnish as desired.

Use clean, uncracked eggs.

*P*ears are available throughout the year, though the best time to eat them is from mid-July through the winter months. America's most popular variety is the Bartlett pear. Other favorites include the Anjou, Bosc, Comice and Seckel. Pears do not ripen on the tree so they are hard when harvested. Ripen them at room temperature until they yield to gentle pressure at the stem end. Pears ripen from the inside out and should not be soft on the outside. When ripe, refrigerate pears right away. For cooking or baking, use firm, slightly underripe pears.

Caramelized Gingersnap Pear Tart

♦ Jane Exline from Milwaukee, Wisconsin was a winner in the Philly "Hall of Fame" Recipe Contest, sponsored by Philadelphia Brand® cream cheese.

Makes 6 to 8 servings

1½ cups gingersnap cookie crumbs
½ cup finely chopped nuts
⅓ cup margarine, melted
2 packages (8 ounces each) cream cheese, softened
¼ cup granulated sugar
2 tablespoons pear nectar or pear brandy
½ teaspoon vanilla
3 ripe pears*
¼ cup packed dark brown sugar
¼ teaspoon ground ginger

Preheat oven to 350°F. Combine crumbs, nuts and margarine in small bowl. Press on bottom and up side of 10-inch quiche dish or 9-inch pie plate. Bake 5 minutes; cool completely on wire rack.

Combine cream cheese and granulated sugar, mixing at medium speed until well blended. Blend in nectar and vanilla. Pour into prepared crust. Cover; refrigerate several hours or overnight.

Just before serving, preheat broiler. Peel and thinly slice pears. Arrange on top of cream cheese mixture. Combine brown sugar and ginger; sprinkle over pears. Broil 3 to 5 minutes or until sugar is melted and bubbly. Serve immediately.

You can substitute 1 (16-ounce) can pear halves, drained and thinly sliced, for fresh pears.

GRAND FINALES

The first meringue was created by a Swiss pastry chef named Gastaparini in the early eighteenth century. He named his new dessert Mehryngen in honor of the snow-clad Alpine village where he spent his boyhood. Gradually the spelling of the word was simplified until it became meringue.

Angel Cream Dessert

♦ Sharon Roach from Lincoln, Illinois was a finalist in the Baked Desserts Using Dairy Foods category at the Illinois State Fair, Springfield, Illinois.

Makes 8 servings

   3 egg whites
 ⅛ teaspoon salt
1½ cups sugar, divided
   1 teaspoon baking powder
1½ teaspoons vanilla, divided
   1 cup crumbled saltine crackers*
 ½ cup chopped pecans
   1 package (3 ounces) cream cheese, softened
   1 cup mini marshmallows
 ½ cup whipped cream
 ½ cup sour cream
 ¼ cup chopped maraschino cherries
   Assorted fresh fruit, for serving

Preheat oven to 350°F. Grease 8-inch round baking pan. Beat egg whites and salt until soft peaks form. Combine 1 cup of the sugar and the baking powder; gradually beat into egg whites. Add 1 teaspoon of the vanilla and beat until stiff and glossy. Fold in crackers and pecans. Pour into prepared pan. Bake 30 minutes. Turn off oven and let stand in oven 10 minutes. Remove from oven and cool completely; center will fall. Remove from pan.

Combine cream cheese with remaining ½ cup sugar and ½ teaspoon vanilla. Gently fold in marshmallows, whipped cream, sour cream and cherries. Spread over cooled base and refrigerate. Serve with fresh fruit if desired.

Saltines should be crumbled with hand so they are not too fine.

Ambrosia Bread Pudding with Whiskey Sauce

♦ Tammy Monjure from Mandeville, Louisiana was a finalist in the Desserts and Candy category of *The Times-Picayune Cookbook* Recipe Contest.

Makes 10 to 12 servings

¾ cup raisins
3 cups evaporated milk
3 eggs
1½ cups sugar
1 cup coarsely chopped pecans
⅔ cup shredded coconut
3 tablespoons butter, melted
2 tablespoons vanilla
1 tablespoon ground cinnamon
2 teaspoons almond extract
1 teaspoon ground nutmeg
1 jar (8 ounces) maraschino cherries, undrained
1 can (11 ounces) mandarin orange segments, undrained
1 loaf whole wheat bread
Whiskey Sauce (recipe follows)

Lightly spray 13×9-inch baking pan with cooking spray. Place raisins in a small bowl and cover with hot water. Let stand 2 to 3 minutes or until plump. Drain. Combine raisins, evaporated milk, eggs, sugar, pecans, coconut, butter, vanilla, cinnamon, almond extract and nutmeg. Add cherries and oranges with liquid. Break bread into pieces and add to milk mixture. Mixture should be moist but not soupy. Pour into prepared pan. Sprinkle with additional coconut if desired. Bake in *unpreheated* 350°F oven 1 hour to 1 hour and 15 minutes or until knife inserted near center comes out clean. Serve with Whiskey Sauce.

Whiskey Sauce: Combine ½ cup melted butter and 1½ cups powdered sugar in medium saucepan. Add 1 egg yolk; mix well with wire whisk. Cook over medium heat, stirring constantly, until thickened. Remove from heat and add ½ cup of bourbon whiskey or almond-flavored liqueur. Let cool sightly.

Toasting Coconut

The full flavor of coconut is released when it is toasted. Spread the coconut in an even layer on a baking sheet and place in a preheated 350°F oven for 8 to 10 minutes. Peek at it after 7 minutes to make sure it is not in any danger of burning. If the coconut is fresh and moist, it will take a little longer to toast into a nice golden color than drier coconut.

Coconut Cheesecake

♦ Betty Rosbottom from Columbus, Ohio was the second place winner in the Sweet category of the International Association of Cooking Professionals Recipe Contest sponsored by Coco Lopez® Cream of Coconut, a product of Borden, Inc.

Makes 10 to 12 servings

1 cup chocolate wafer cookie crumbs
   (about 18 wafers)
1 cup finely chopped pecans
2 tablespoons sugar
¼ cup margarine or butter, melted
3 packages (8 ounces each) cream cheese,
   softened
3 eggs
2 tablespoons all-purpose flour
1 can (15 ounces) cream of coconut
1 can (3½ ounces) flaked coconut (1⅓ cups),
   toasted, divided
Whipped cream, for garnish

Preheat oven to 300°F. Combine crumbs, pecans and sugar; stir in margarine. Press firmly on bottom of 9-inch springform pan. Beat cheese at high speed with electric mixer until fluffy. Add eggs and flour, beating until smooth. Gradually beat in cream of coconut. Stir in ¾ cup of the toasted coconut.

Pour into prepared pan. Bake 1 hour and 10 to 15 minutes or until cake springs back when lightly touched (center will be soft). Carefully loosen cheesecake from edge of pan with knife tip. Cool on wire rack; refrigerate until firm. Remove side of pan. Spoon or pipe whipped cream around outside edge of cheesecake. Sprinkle remaining toasted coconut inside whipped cream border.

In French, "coeur à la crème" means "heart with cream." Coeur à la crème is a classic dessert often made in specially shaped wicker baskets or heart-shaped porcelain molds with holes in the bottom. After the cheese mixture is placed in the cheesecloth-lined baskets or molds, the holes allow the liquid (whey) in the cheeses to drain off. You can find coeur à la crème molds in specialty food shops.

Coeur à la Crème

♦ James St. Clair was a prize winner at the March of Dimes Gourmet Gala in Boston, Massachusetts.

Makes 6 servings

1 package (8 ounces) cream cheese, softened
1 cup small curd cottage cheese
1 cup whipping cream
⅓ cup powdered sugar
2 teaspoons vanilla
1 pint fresh strawberries, hulled
2 tablespoons orange-flavored liqueur

Blend cream cheese and cottage cheese in food processor or blender. In small chilled bowl, whip cream with sugar and vanilla until stiff peaks form. Fold whipped cream into cheese mixture. Line 6 coeur à la crème molds with moist cheesecloth. Divide cheese mixture evenly between molds. Place on platter and refrigerate until thoroughly chilled.

Process strawberries and liqueur in food processor or blender until puréed. To serve, spoon strawberry sauce onto small dessert plates; invert each coeur à la crème onto sauce.

azelnuts or filberts have thin brown skins that are often removed before eating. Try this method to remove the skins and to toast the nuts at the same time. Place the nuts on a baking sheet and bake them in a preheated 350°F oven for 8 to 10 minutes or until the skins begin to flake off. Remove them from the oven, wrap them in a heavy towel and rub them against the towel to remove as much of the skins as possible.

Chocolate Mousse Espresso with Hazelnut Brittle

♦ Jonathan A. Fox from Wheeling, Illinois was a prize winner in the Knox® Unflavored Gelatine Recipe Contest, sponsored by Thomas J. Lipton, Inc., at The Culinary Institute of America, Hyde Park, New York.

Makes about 10 servings

   Hazelnut Brittle (recipe follows)
 2 envelopes Knox® Unflavored Gelatine
 ¾ cup sugar, divided
 4 teaspoons instant espresso coffee
2¾ cups milk
 12 squares (1 ounce each) semisweet chocolate
1½ cups heavy cream
 ⅔ cup hazelnuts, toasted, skinned and chopped
2½ cups chocolate cookie wafer crumbs

Prepare Hazelnut Brittle; set aside. Mix gelatine with ½ cup of the sugar and the coffee in medium saucepan; blend in milk and let stand 1 minute. Stir over low heat until gelatine is completely dissolved, about 5 minutes. Add chocolate and continue heating, stirring constantly, until chocolate is melted. Using wire whisk, beat until chocolate is thoroughly blended. Pour into large bowl and refrigerate, stirring occasionally, until mixture mounds slightly when dropped from spoon.

In medium bowl, whip cream with remaining ¼ cup sugar. Reserve ½ cup of the cream for garnish. Fold remaining cream mixture into gelatine mixture. Combine hazelnuts and cookie crumbs. Alternately layer gelatine mixture with hazelnut mixture in dessert dishes. Refrigerate at least 30 minutes. Garnish each dish with pieces of hazelnut brittle and reserved whipped cream.

Hazelnut Brittle: Toast, skin and chop 1 cup hazelnuts. Place 1 cup sugar in large skillet over medium heat. As sugar begins to melt, gently tilt skillet until sugar is completely melted and golden brown. Stir in hazelnuts. Quickly pour onto greased baking sheet; do not spread. Let stand until cooled and hardened. Break into pieces.

Every April in Vermont, when the snow is often still thick on the ground, a great maple festival takes place. There are maple-glazed doughnuts, maple-sugar candy, pancakes drenched in maple syrup and as much maple fudge to eat as a body can bear. And, of course, there's a cooking contest where the winner is crowned Mrs. Maple, the Maple Queen.

Maple Sweetheart

♦ Jeannine Dandurand was the winner of the Mrs. Maple award at the Vermont Maple Festival, St. Albans, Vermont.

Makes about 10 servings

  1 package (3 ounces) ladyfingers, split
  2 tablespoons unflavored gelatin
  ¼ cup cold water
  ½ cup real maple syrup
  5 eggs*
  1½ cups heavy cream
    Dark brown sugar and whipped cream,
      for garnish

Line sides of 9-inch springform pan with ladyfingers. Sprinkle gelatin over water in small saucepan; let stand 1 minute. Stir over low heat until gelatin is completely dissolved, about 5 minutes.

Bring maple syrup in heavy saucepan to a boil; continue boiling until it reaches 230°F on a candy thermometer. Meanwhile, beat eggs in large bowl until light and fluffy. Gradually add hot syrup in thin stream, beating until mixture starts to cool. Stir in gelatin. Refrigerate about 30 minutes or until mixture mounds slightly when dropped from spoon.

In medium bowl, whip cream until stiff peaks form; fold into thickened mixture. Pour into prepared pan and refrigerate 2 hours until firm. To serve, remove side of pan and garnish with brown sugar and additional whipped cream.

*Use clean, uncracked eggs.

Making Vanilla Sugar

To make vanilla sugar, place 1 or 2 vanilla beans in a small canister of granulated sugar. Keep the canister tightly closed for a few weeks or until the sugar is infused with the flavor of vanilla. You can continue to replenish the sugar in the canister until the beans lose their flavoring power. Substitute vanilla sugar for plain sugar whenever a sweet vanilla flavor is desired.

Crème Brûlée

♦ Sue Wylie was a prize winner at the March of Dimes Gourmet Gala in Lexington, Kentucky.

Makes 6 servings

2 cups whipping cream
1 tablespoon vanilla sugar
4 egg yolks, beaten
¾ cup sieved brown sugar*

Preheat oven to 350°F. Heat cream in top of covered double boiler over hot, not boiling, water 5 to 7 minutes or until hot but not scalding. Remove from heat and add vanilla sugar; stir until dissolved. Gradually beat egg yolks into hot cream. Pour into 7½-inch pie plate or 6 small ovenproof bowls. Set plate or bowls in pan of hot water. Bake on middle rack of oven 50 to 60 minutes or until set. (The custard may still look runny, but it will continue to set up after being removed from oven.) Refrigerate until well chilled.

Preheat broiler. Sprinkle ¼-inch-thick layer of brown sugar over top of custard. Broil 6 inches from heat, rotating occasionally, to brown the sugar evenly. A fine, dark golden crust will form. Serve immediately to enjoy the hot and cold contrasts or refrigerate and serve cold.

To measure sieved brown sugar, press sugar through sieve, letting it fall lightly into measuring cup.

Note: Since the custard should be very cold when placed under the broiler, it is best to make it the day before you plan to serve it.

Cream of coconut is made by pressing the white meat of tree-ripened coconuts into a thick liquid. The liquid is then processed into a creamy consistency. It is available in supermarkets in the beverage, baking or specialty foods sections.

Coconut-Orange Soufflé

◆ Bonnie Aeschliman from Wichita, Kansas won first place in the Sweet category of the International Association of Cooking Professionals Recipe Contest sponsored by Coco Lopez® Cream of Coconut, a product of Borden, Inc.

Makes 8 to 10 servings

2 envelopes unflavored gelatin
½ cup water
4 eggs,* separated
½ cup sugar, divided
1 can (15 ounces) cream of coconut
1 cup pineapple juice
¼ cup crème de cacao (optional)
¼ cup frozen orange juice concentrate, thawed
1 tablespoon bottled lemon juice
½ teaspoon grated orange peel (optional)
1 cup whipping cream
Whipped cream and orange peel, for garnish

Sprinkle gelatin over water; set aside. In small saucepan, beat egg yolks and ¼ cup of the sugar. Cook over low heat, stirring constantly until thickened. Add gelatin mixture; stir, over low heat, until gelatin is completely dissolved, about 3 minutes. Combine gelatin mixture, cream of coconut, pineapple juice, crème de cacao, orange juice concentrate, lemon juice and orange peel in large bowl. Refrigerate, stirring occasionally, until mixture mounds slightly when dropped from spoon, about 45 minutes.

Beat egg whites until soft peaks form. Gradually add remaining ¼ cup sugar beating until stiff and glossy. Fold into gelatin mixture. Whip cream until soft peaks form; fold into gelatin mixture. Tape a 3-inch-wide waxed paper "collar" around rim of 1½-quart soufflé dish. Pour mixture into prepared dish. Refrigerate 3 hours or until set. Remove collar; garnish with whipped cream and orange peel.

*Use clean, uncracked eggs.
Note: To make waxed paper "collar" see tip on page 54.

INDEX